Newbridge Discovery Links®

Paul Pascal

Newbridge

A Haights Cross Communications ✦ Company

Ice on Earth
ISBN: 1-4007-3680-3

Program Author: Dr. Brenda Parkes, Literacy Expert
Content Reviewer: Dr. Roger G. Barry, Professor of Geography and Director, National Snow and Ice Data
  Center (NSIDC) and World Data Center for Glaciology, University of Colorado, Boulder, CO

Written by Paul Pascal
Design assistance by Kirchoff/Wohlberg, Inc.

Newbridge Educational Publishing
11 East 26th Street, New York, NY 10010
www.newbridgeonline.com

Cover photograph: Hikers climbing the Baltoro Glacier, Pakistan
Table of Contents photograph: Iceberg off the coast of Antarctica

Photo Credits
Cover: Peter Cole/ImageState; Table of Contents page: Colin Monteath/ImageState; pages 4–5: (background) MODIS/NASA; page 5: Maria Stenzel/National Geographic; page 6: Macduff Everton/Corbis; page 7: (background) MODIS/NASA; page 8: Thomas Ligon/arc Software Simulations/Photo Researchers; page 9: Darwin Wiggett/Corbis; pages 10–11: Galen Rowell/Corbis; page 12: Yann Arthus-Bertrand/Corbis; page 13: Paul A. Souders/Corbis; page 14: Hans Strand/Corbis; page 15: David Meunch/Corbis; page 16: Hedgehog House/ImageState; page 17: (top left) Galen Rowell/Corbis, (top right) Bernhard Edmaier/Science Photo Library/Photo Researchers, (bottom) Brock May/Photo Researchers; page 18: Galen Rowell/Corbis; page 19: Gordon R. Gainer/Corbis; page 20: Mark A. Chappell/Animals Animals; page 21: Greg Dimijian/Photo Researchers; page 22: AP/Wide World Photos; page 24: AP/Wide World Photos, (background) MODIS/NASA; page 25: MODIS/NASA; page 26: Joseph Sohm/Corbis; page 27: AP/Wide World Photos; page 29: Galen Rowell/Corbis; page 30: Winifred Wisniewski/Corbis; page 32: (background) MODIS/NASA

Illustrations by Mike DiGiorgio pages 7, 10, 23

10 9 8 7 6 5 4 3 2 1

GUIDED READING
LEVEL **R**

Table of Contents

AMAZING ICE

Imagine spending two months camping in a place without running water or electricity, and thousands of miles away from the nearest town or city. Imagine being in a place where the average temperature is about 5°F and where a blizzard can keep you trapped in your tent for days at a time.

That's just what teams of scientists do every year. Starting at McMurdo Station near the coast of Antarctica, scientists travel towards the South Pole.

As they travel, the scientists take samples of the Antarctic ice. Later, each ice sample will be carefully studied and analyzed in a laboratory.

Why spend so much time in the extreme cold of Antarctica collecting and studying ice samples? What's so interesting about ice anyway?

Scientists use high-tech drills to extract ice core samples—long rods of ice. By studying the samples, they learn about Earth's history and climate.

Scientists are interested in ice because it's a powerful force that has important effects on life on Earth. About 10 percent of our planet is covered by ice. Ice plays a role in our global climate and weather. It shapes our land. Ice is also one of Earth's storage systems for water. Much of Earth's freshwater is stored in ice.

Lakes, hills, and other landforms were carved out of the earth by ice.

WHERE'S THE ICE?

When seen from space, Earth appears blue, green, brown, and white. The white is the ice that covers parts of the land and water. Ice covers large areas of land and caps the highest mountains.

What causes ice to form in certain places on Earth? The answer has to do with how the sun heats the planet. The more sunlight a place gets, the warmer it is. The less sunlight a place gets, the colder. The area around the **equator** is the warmest because it receives the most direct sunlight.

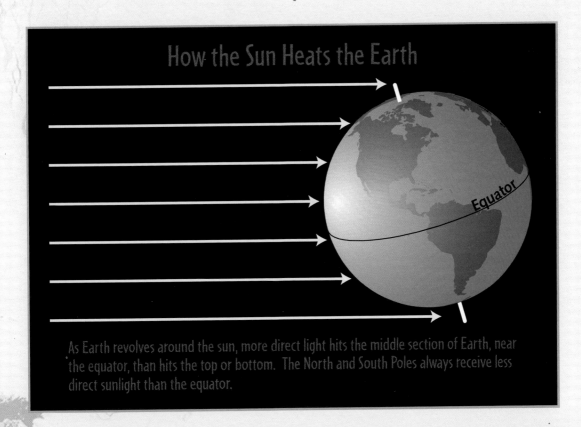

How the Sun Heats the Earth

Equator

As Earth revolves around the sun, more direct light hits the middle section of Earth, near the equator, than hits the top or bottom. The North and South Poles always receive less direct sunlight than the equator.

The polar regions—lands north of the **Arctic Circle** and south of the **Antarctic Circle**—are far colder because they get less direct sunlight. In fact, during the winter months, the sun doesn't shine at all in these places. Because of the extreme cold, most of our planet's ice is found in the polar regions. Ice also forms high in mountain ranges where it's much colder than at lower elevations.

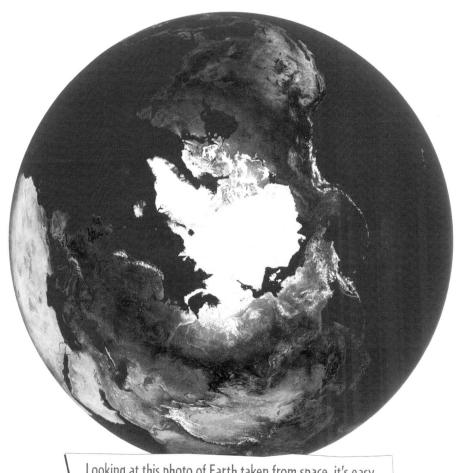

Looking at this photo of Earth taken from space, it's easy to spot our planet's icy Arctic.

Ice forms in the polar regions and at high elevations because the snow that falls in these regions tends to stay put. The temperatures are so cold that the snow never melts completely—not even during the short summers. Instead, it builds up over time. As new snow falls, it presses down on the layers of snow underneath. Over many years, the pressure squeezes the particles of snow together, gradually turning them into ice.

This ice is called **glacial ice.** Glacial ice takes many forms, including **ice sheets** that cover large areas, and **mountain glaciers.**

The temperature always drops as you move up a mountain.

An Ice-Covered Continent

Most of the world's ice is found in Antarctica, the huge, frozen continent surrounded by the Antarctic Ocean. The entire continent is covered by two massive ice sheets.

These two ice sheets cover almost all the land. They cover whole mountains so that only the peaks break through the ice. A person at the South Pole is standing on a sheet of ice that is almost two miles deep. The ice at the bottom of the ice sheet is a million years old.

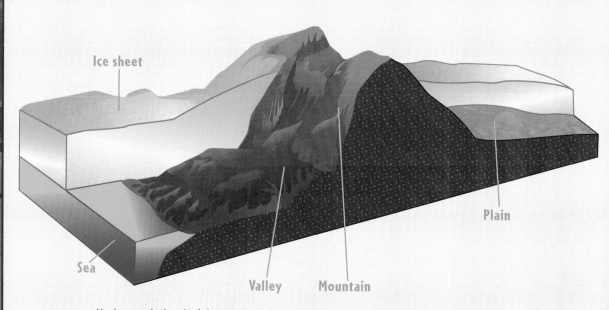

Underneath the thick layer of ice, Antarctica has mountains, plains, and valleys.

These huge sheets of ice move. The ice sheets advance slowly from the center towards the edge of the continent. In fact, the sign that marks the official South Pole must be adjusted each year as the giant ice sheets slide over the land.

Antarctica's climate makes it uninhabitable. There are no permanent residents on Antarctica. Only about 1,000 people spend the winter in Antarctica.

In the Antarctic, many icebergs have flat tops and look a lot like floating pieces of a huge sheet cake. One giant iceberg was the size of Delaware.

The Antarctic ice extends over parts of the ocean as well, in sheets called **ice shelves.** The largest one is about the size of Texas! In spots, it is more than 1,200 meters thick.

When chunks of ice shelves break off and float away, the pieces are called **icebergs.** This process is called calving. The calving of an iceberg is anything but a quiet event! Loud rumbling, hissing, and cracking sounds indicate that the ice is about to break. Once floating, the iceberg may grumble and moan for a long time, causing some icebergs to be called "growlers."

Icebergs help to replace water lost through evaporation. As they melt, they release freshwater into the ocean.

Wind and water can carve icebergs into amazing shapes.

Sea Ice and Mountain Glaciers

The Arctic is another icy place on our planet. But the ice at the top of the world is different. Unlike Antarctica, the Arctic is not a continent. Most of the Arctic is ocean surrounded by land. In the Arctic, the largest expanse of ice is over the ocean. It is made of frozen seawater, called **sea ice.**

Sea ice is different from glacial ice, because it is frozen ocean, or salt water. While freshwater freezes at 32°F, salt water has to be colder to freeze—28.6°F.

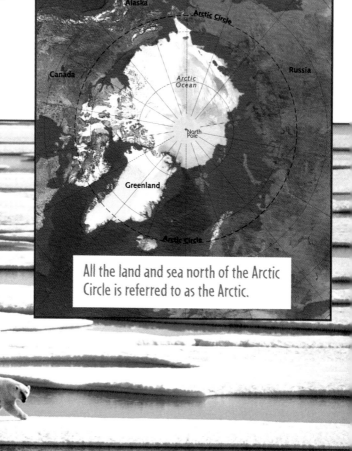

All the land and sea north of the Arctic Circle is referred to as the Arctic.

Polar bears roam the sea ice, hunting the seals that swim beneath the ice.

In the wintertime, the sea ice on the Arctic Ocean reaches all the way to the coastlines. In the summer, some of the ice melts and breaks into pieces called **ice floes.**

The land above the Arctic Circle is also icy. It is home to many of the world's mountain glaciers. There are also glaciers, that flow through mountain valleys, and others that flow across flat plains.

The Lamplugh Glacier in Glacier Bay National Park is just one of the more than 5,000 glaciers in Alaska.

Iceberg Ahead!

Icebergs come in amazing sizes, shapes, and even colors—and all of these characteristics are clues to where the iceberg is from, how old it is, and more!

Some ice looks blue! This is because the ice is very old and, over time, pressure has pushed out all of the air. Without air pockets, the ice reflects light differently and appears blue. Algae can make an iceberg look green or red.

Icebergs float so that there is always about one-eighth above the surface of the water and seven-eighths below. As the top melts, some of the ice below the surface rises up. If you look closely, you may see lines going across icebergs that show previous water levels.

Icebergs that break off from mountain glaciers are a different shape than the ones that break off an ice shelf. They are more jagged and tend to have points and peaks at the top.

Only the tip of an iceberg shows above the surface of the ocean. The larger part is hidden below and that makes it very hazardous to ships. The jagged, underwater edges can tear a hole in the side of even the biggest ship if it gets too close. The sinking of the *Titanic* in 1912 was caused by an iceberg.

CHILLING THE PLANET

The icy North and South Poles have been described as air conditioners for our planet because they help keep the planet cool. Earth is constantly being heated by the sun. Most of that heat is absorbed. But the ice in the polar regions reflects the sun's heat instead of absorbing it. This helps to lower the temperature on Earth. If the ice sheets and glaciers did not exist, the average global temperature could increase by about 15°F.

The average winter temperature at the South Pole research station is about –70°F. Temperatures in the Arctic don't drop that low, because the Arctic ice is much thinner and covers warmer ocean water.

The polar regions help to keep air moving around the planet. Warm tropical air above the equator rises and moves toward the poles. Cold polar air flows south.

The same thing happens in the ocean. Warm water rises and cool water slips in underneath. The movement of cold and warm water helps create ocean currents. This circulation of both air and water helps to distribute heat around the planet.

People in the northern United States get a taste of the Arctic climate when the polar jet stream, a powerful current of wind, dips to the south. This frigid wind brings bitterly cold weather.

All of these systems are connected, and a change in one will cause a change in the other. For example, each spring, the sea ice over the Arctic Ocean breaks up. A mass of this ice melts off the coast of Greenland and the cold water sinks. Some of this cold water flows south through the Atlantic Ocean. A change in the amount of sea ice could affect this ocean current, and a change in the current could affect global weather.

Tiny plants and animals called plankton live in the cold ocean waters near the polar regions. Plankton is food for some whales and many other sea creatures. The circulation of cold water helps distribute plankton through the oceans.

SHAPING THE EARTH

Glaciers are often described as rivers of ice. That's because all glaciers move. Glaciers flow like very slow-moving rivers. Many flow down the sides of mountains, but some move through valleys or across plains. Most glaciers move slowly—at a rate of no more than a few centimeters a day. Some, however, are known as "galloping glaciers" because they move at a more rapid rate.

Several factors cause a glacier to advance, or move forward. One is the slope of the land underneath—gravity helps pull a glacier downward.

How do you think this glacier affects the land as it flows?

Visitors to the Kenai Fjords National Park in Alaska can actually climb to the top of Exit Glacier.

Once a glacier begins to move, the friction between its bottom and the ground melts the bottom layer of ice, putting a thin layer of water between the glacier and the ground. This gives the glacier a slippery surface to glide on.

Glaciers also **retreat.** A glacier doesn't actually move backwards. What happens is that the edges of the glacier melt, making the glacier appear to pull back.

Glaciers have a great impact on the land as they advance and retreat. Like enormous bulldozers, they gouge huge holes in the earth. They chip rock away from mountain peaks and carve out mountain valleys. You can see the deep scratches they have made in some rocks.

When they retreat, glaciers leave behind reminders of their visit. They drop loads of rock and other debris in ridges and mounds called **moraines.** Long Island and Cape Cod were both created by huge expanses of moraine left by glaciers. Some lakes were created when holes dug out by glaciers filled with water.

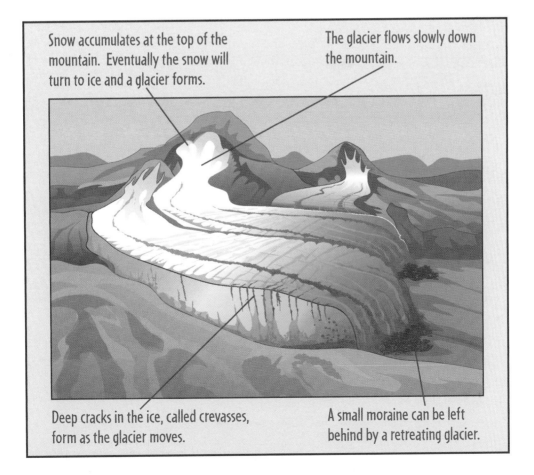

Snow accumulates at the top of the mountain. Eventually the snow will turn to ice and a glacier forms.

The glacier flows slowly down the mountain.

Deep cracks in the ice, called crevasses, form as the glacier moves.

A small moraine can be left behind by a retreating glacier.

AN ICY PAST...AND FUTURE?

Glaciers advance and retreat. Giant icebergs break off and eventually melt away. Sea ice melts and re-forms every year. These changes are always taking place. But in the history of our planet, there have been far more dramatic changes in the earth's ice.

Scientists believe that at one time the whole planet was warmer and relatively ice-free. Then something—perhaps a change in the sun's output of heat—caused the climate to change. Earth had entered an **ice age,** a period lasting millions of years during which the temperature dropped drastically and massive glaciers and ice sheets formed.

Ice covered about a third of the planet, including much of North America, Europe, Asia, and the oceans. There have been at least five ice ages in the history of Earth, the last one ending about 10,000 years ago.

The bones of a prehistoric mammoth from the last ice age were discovered in California in 1999. Discoveries like this one help scientists learn about the plants and animals that lived in a place thousands of years ago.

The Great Lakes were carved out of the earth by glaciers retreating during the last ice age.

During past ice ages, enormous glaciers advanced over Earth's surface, changing its shape and wiping out some of the plants and animals. During the periods between ice ages, the ice retreats. Ocean levels rise as the ice melts, large holes left behind by glaciers fill with water, and many plants and animals return to the land and oceans.

Cooling and Warming Trends

It is possible, according to some scientists, that we might be living in a period between ice ages. A change in Earth's orbit around the sun, for example, could cause a change in the climate. Of course, it would take many thousands of years for the earth to cool enough to cause a major drop in temperature and a big increase in the total amount of ice.

But there is also evidence that a completely opposite effect is underway—**global warming.** This warming trend is the result of more and more carbon dioxide being released into the air when coal, oil, and other fuels are burned. The carbon dioxide holds heat, and this warms the blanket of air that covers the planet. This, in turn, warms the oceans and the land, causing the climate to warm up.

Plants can grow inside a greenhouse even in winter because the glass covering the greenhouse lets light through but prevents heat from escaping. Carbon dioxide and other "greenhouse" gases act in the same way.

There's evidence that Antarctica was once a warmer place. Coal deposits found in the ground under the ice are proof that plants lived and died there–their decaying roots, leaves, and stems eventually turned into coal.

In recent years, scientists have noticed that many of the world's glaciers seem to be melting at a faster rate. This might be a sign that Earth is getting warmer. An ice cap in Iceland has been retreating about one meter each year. Mountain glaciers in the Himalayas have flooded lakes because they are melting so fast. Huge icebergs have been breaking off an ice shelf in Antarctica.

Is the climate on Earth really heating up or are we entering another ice age? When will we feel the effects? How will our planet change?

Looking for Answers

Scientists are trying to find the answers to all these questions. Satellites take photographs that show how much snow and ice cover there is. Meteorologists at weather stations in the Arctic and on Antarctica are gathering information to build a record of weather over time. These methods help scientists monitor what is happening to glaciers and to our climate today.

Scientists are also trying to find answers in the ice. That's why scientists from the International Trans-Antarctic Scientific Expedition and other groups working in the Arctic are extracting ice core samples. These long cylinders of ice are like frozen time lines. The ice at the bottom has been on Earth for thousands, maybe millions, of years. The ice at the top is relatively new. In each layer are tiny bits of all the things that existed at the time— including dust and **fossils.**

To the trained eye, the ice helps tell the story of life on Earth long ago. In the ice, scientists can find evidence of how Earth's climate and atmosphere have changed over time. In fact, from evidence in the ice, scientists have been able to confirm volcanic eruptions in the past that, until now, were just the stuff of ancient stories and legends.

Scientists are launching this balloon to test the air above Antarctica. What do you think they can learn?

Ice core samples, satellite photographs, and new climate data will help scientists make predictions about what is happening to our planet today and what might happen in the future.

Earth is always changing. Its air, land, and water all move and flow in different ways. Some changes happen over weeks, months, or years. Other changes happen over hundreds and thousands of years.

Ice is one of the features of our planet that is always changing, and as it changes, it shapes and affects our world.

GLOSSARY

Antarctic Circle: an imaginary circle around the bottom of the earth. South of the Antarctic Circle there is at least one day of total darkness and one day of total daylight each year.

Arctic Circle: an imaginary circle around the top of the earth. North of the Circle there is at least one day of total darkness and one day of total daylight each year.

equator: an imaginary line around the middle of the earth that divides the earth into the Northern and Southern Hemispheres

fossil: hardened remains or traces of plant or animal life from long ago, preserved in the earth

glacial ice: ice formed by snow that gets compacted over many years

global warming: an increase in the earth's average temperature that causes changes in climate

ice age: a cold period characterized by the formation of a large number of glaciers that covered much of the earth's surface

ice floes: a large flat mass of floating ice

ice sheet: an enormous mass of glacial ice that covers the land

ice shelf: a portion of an ice sheet that spreads out over water

iceberg: a floating chunk of ice that has broken off from the end of a glacier or ice shelf.

moraine: a mound or ridge created by a glacier pushing gravel and sand together

mountain glacier: a huge mass of ice that forms in a high mountainous region and can extend over several peaks or mountain ranges

retreat: when the edge of a glacier melts, making the glacier appear to move backwards

sea ice: frozen seawater

INDEX

WEBSITES

www.secretsoftheice.org

nsidc.org/glaciers/

www.glacier.rice.edu